SHRI VANDE BHARTI

Shri Suktam Havan Vidhi

1

Preface

"Su" combined with "ktam" means "Well Said" in Sanskrit. A "Suktam" is a collection of the most important verses from the Vedas, sung by Rishis (sages) in praise of a single deity. This booklet focuses on Shri Suktam, dedicated to Goddess Mahalakshmi, the deity of Wealth and Prosperity.

Benefits of Shri Suktam

Dedicated practice of Shri Suktam is believed to:

- Fulfill one's wishes
- Bring all-round success in life
- Bestow wealth, prosperity, prestige, health, family, friends, associates, and fame.

The Vedas are considered the most sacred texts in Hinduism and are revered as the abode of Gods. They provide insights into the past, present, and future.

The Four Vedas:

1. Rig Veda
2. Yajur Veda
3. Sama Veda
4. Atharva Veda (composed later by sage Vedavyas, combining verses from the original three)

Shri Suktam is found in both the Rig Veda and Atharva Veda. It is known to bestow complete progress through the grace of Goddess Mahalakshmi.

In today's busy world, it's challenging for individuals to study the Vedas in depth. This booklet is the first in a series that aims to:

- Enable readers to perform a Homam (havan) by themselves
- Make Vedic wisdom more accessible to modern practitioners

Ashta Lakshmi

These are the 8 facets of Mahalakshmi, known as Ashta Lakshmi.

1. Aadi Lakshmi—the primal mother goddess
2. Dhan Lakshmi—goddess of material wealth
3. Dhanya Lakshmi—goddess of good harvest and grains
4. Gaja Lakshmi—goddess of power and strength
5. Santaan Lakshmi—goddess of off-springs and progeny
6. Veer Lakshmi—goddess of courage and strength
7. Vijay Lakshmi—goddess of victory

8. Aishwarya Lakshmi—goddess of comfort and luxury

Performing a havan (fire ritual) with this 5,000 year old hymn called Shri Suktam every week, preferably on Fridays, brings miraculous results. But, to achieve the desired results and grace you must know the meanings and recite the verses correctly.

2

Havan

Havan, as it is known in Northern India and as homa or homam, in Southern India is one and the same; it is derived from the root word 'hu', meaning "to offer" or "to present" in Sanskrit—a ritual wherein oblations are offered into the fire to appease the deities.

Fire being one of the five main elements is considered to be the sacrosanct element of a Havan or Homa, who is responsible for delivering the offerings that are made into the sacred fire during a Havan to the deities.

In addition to appeasing the deities, a Havan is said to purify the environment and drive away negative energies and benefit all present at the Havan ceremony.

We perform Havan in a Havan Kund made of metal or a fire pit made of bricks depending on how big the ritual ceremony is; we decorate the ground with colorful flowers and the items used in performing Havan are a special mixture of medicinal herbs, roots, dry fruits, cow-dung cakes or wood and ghee (clarified butter) which are offered as oblations into the Havan Kund fire accompanied by chanting Sanskrit Mantras.

Enhancing the Experience

- Invite guests: Friends, neighbors, and relatives
- Distribute materials: Share copies of the ritual booklet if available

Encourage participation:

- Ask attendees to recite mantras
- Guide them to mimic the oblation-pouring gesture when "Swāhā" is pronounced
- Immersion: This participatory approach enhances the ritual's efficacy and creates a more engaging experience

By following these guidelines, you can create a meaningful and inclusive Havan ceremony that honors tradition while fostering community engagement.

Please view a dedicated FAQ playlist on our Youtube channel at www.youtube.com/@vandeshri if you still have any questions and then email them to shrivandebharti@gmail.com

3

Additional Information

Types of Havan Kunds

As per the Scriptures, a Havan Kund's shapes and sizes vary as per the ritual and the intent for which the Havan is being conducted and the deity being invoked.

You may have seen the Square Shaped Havan Kund as it is primarily used in the rituals. The square shape Havan Kund is also called as Chaturastra Kund or the Kund design made with 4 equal sides.

- Chaturastra Kund - Square shaped Havan Kund is for the accomplishment of all wishes.
- Yoni Kund - Heart shaped Havan Kund is for attracting love and getting a child.
- Ardha Chandra Kund - Crescent moon shaped Havan Kund

is to resolve marital conflicts, where both husband and wife offer oblations together.

- Trikon Kund - Triangle shaped Havan Kund resembling a bow & arrow is for defeating enemies.
- Vrut Kund - Circular in shape is for world peace and general welfare.
- Pushtrkon Kund - Star shaped Havan Kund for victory over seen or unseen enemies.
- Padma Kund - Lotus shaped Havan Kund is primarily made to attract wealth.

Types Of Havans (Rituals)

There are many Havans for various intents, here are the few commonly performed Havans:—

- Mahalakshmi havan
- Rudra Havan pooja
- Navagraha havan
- Nakshatra havan
- Maha Mrityunjaya havan
- Sudarshan havan
- Saraswati havan
- Lakshmi Narasimha havan
- Lakshmi Narayana Havan
- Chandi havan
- Dhanvantari havan
- Gayatri havan
- Santana Gopala havan

The Benefits Of A Havan

Havan benefits our body, mind, soul, and the environment, some of which have been proven by scientific evaluation.

Various gasses produced during Havan decompose the poisonous gasses liberating free oxygen and other useful products acting as disinfectants. A scientist named Trelle of France found that a gas named "formic aldehyde" is generated when dried twigs from mango trees are used in a Havan; destroying harmful bacteria in the atmosphere.

Havan strengthens the mental abilities and induces peace, good health, prosperity, clarity of thought, and improved usage of mental abilities.

When Should A Havan Be Performed?

Ideally, Havan should be performed daily or at least once per week along with all the members of the family. It should be performed as per the Choghadiya Muhurat (auspicious time), covered later in this book.

Asana

Asana means the seat on which one sits while performing a Havan—it is a very important part of the ritual and care should be taken when selecting an Asana. Performing any ritual without an Asana brings misfortune.

Types of Asanas

Silk, woollen, Deer skin, Kusha (grass that grows near river banks)—always use a square or a rectangular Asana.

Kusha is easily available in India and used in temperate climatic conditions, but Woolen Asana is best for people staying in colder climatic conditions.

Typically a ring also has to be worn made from Kusha for performing a Havan, but it can be substituted with a gold or a silver ring; worn on the ring finger of the right hand.

The Asana should be either Yellow or Red—for Shri Suktam—Yellow is the preferred color.

Tilak

Tilak is the colored paste or ash applied on the forehead, more specifically in between eyebrows - Our bodies are a bundle of 72,000 nerves (Nadis) and there are many plexes through which these nerves pass, of these plexes there are 7 major plexes also known as

Kundalini Chakras

Energy flows through these Nadis (Astral nerves) and distribute the life-force throughout the body. The plexes in between the eyebrows, where Nadis come together is

Ajna Chakra

Applying Tilak at this point prevents the negative energy being projected by others to enter our bodies.

4

Kalawa

Also known as Raksha Sutra, is a tricolor ceremonial thread, which is tied on the right wrist before every auspicious task - if you already have one, then you can either keep that old one or change it with a new one.

It has to be wrapped around your right wrist nine times - males and spinster females wear it on their right wrist and married females wear it on their left wrist, by doing this you get the blessings of Brahma, Vishnu, and Mahesh as well as their spouses the trinity Goddesses Mahasaraswati, Mahalakshmi, and Mahaparvati respectively.

Recite this mantra as you tie it: -

yaina bādhō balirājā dānavēndrō mahābalaḥ tēnātavam
pratibad'dhanāmi rakśē mācala mācalāḥ|

Meaning: Raja Bali, Danavendra Mahabali is committed to protect the life and property of the one who has this Kalawa tied on his wrist.

12

5

Mudra

Mudras are symbolic "gestures" often practiced with the hands and fingers. They facilitate the flow of energy in the subtle body and enhance one's journey within.

If more than one person is actively participating in a Havan, then one can offer Ghee as the oblations and another can offer 'samagri', which is a mixture of fragrant twigs, herbs, roots, dry-fruits etc.

The person offering Ghee does so with a spoon, but the one offering samagri uses the right hand particularly the forming a 'Mrig' meaning Deer mudra which is picking up the samagri with thumb, middle finger, and ring finger.

The other hand should form Chin Mudra, which is done by gently tucking the tip of the index finger under the tip of the thumb, keeping the remaining three fingers lightly extended, palms facing upwards.

6

Japa

'Japa' means murmured prayer.

Japa is an ancient practice in which a mantra or the name of a deity is recited either silently or aloud. The Sanskrit word is derived from the root word:—"jap".

Japa can be performed in three ways—meditatively within the mind, without uttering a word or moving your tongue; by 'whispering' and finally in a low voice that can be heard only by oneself.

Many people prefer to perform a japa once or more than once daily; and Havan once a week—as japa is convenient and requires relatively less preparation than a havan.
   Also, japa is performed for one's own benefit, whereas Havan benefits the whole family and friends present at the ceremony.

You can perform a japa daily instead of a Havan—the process remains the same, except you need 108 bead mala for a japa.

There is a mantra on my Youtube channel, which has a musical score and is repeated 108 times, you can play it while doing japa.

7

Choghadiya Muhurat

Every religious and auspicious ceremony has to be done at a proper time which is called Muhurat and is chosen scientifically as per the locations of the planets, Sunrise and Sunset.

Each day is divided between Sunrise to Sunset into 30 Ghati and into 8 phases, which results in 8 Choghadiya Muhurat during the daytime and 8 Choghadiya Muhurat during the nighttime. As each Choghadiya Muhurat is approximately 4 Ghati; Choghadiya = Cho (four) + Ghadiya (Ghati) also known as Chaturshtika Muhurta.

Each phase is of one hour and twenty-four minutes; the good muhurats during every 12-hour period are:- Amrit, Shubh, Labh and Char and the bad muhurats are:-Rog, Kaal, and Udveg. In addition, there could be any of the following evil omens that overlap the auspicious phase known as Vaar Vela, Kaal Vela, Rahu Kaal and Kaal Ratri.

If auspicious Choghadiya overlaps with Rahu Kala, Vara Vela,

Kala Vela and Kala Ratri—which are highly malefic for any auspicious activity; such overlapping Choghadiya Muhurta must be avoided and we should postpone the activity to a favorable Choghadiya Muhurta.

The first Muhurta on each day is ruled by its celestial lord. For example, Sunday's first Choghadiya Muhurta is ruled by the Sun, followed by Venus, Mercury, Moon, Saturn, Jupiter and Mars respectively. The day's ruling planet also rules the last Muhurta of that day.

Hence the effect of each division, either bad or good, is marked based on the ruling planet. In Vedic Astrology, the time under the influence of Venus, Mercury, Moon and Jupiter is considered auspicious while the time under the influence of Sun, Mars and Saturn is considered inauspicious.

Here are the activities that can be performed under various Choghadiya Muhurat and their results:—

Udveg Choghadiya

The Sun is considered a malefic planet in Vedic astrology. Hence the time under the influence of it is usually considered inauspicious and marked as Udveg. However, for government-related work, Udveg Choghadiya is considered good.

Char Choghadiya

Venus is considered a benign planet in Vedic astrology. Hence the time under the influence of it is considered auspicious and marked as Char or Chanchal. Due to the moving nature of the Venus, Char Choghadiya is considered most appropriate for traveling purposes.

Labh Choghadiya

Mercury is considered a benign planet in Vedic astrology. Hence the time under the influence of it is considered auspicious and marked as Labh. Labh Choghadiya is considered most appropriate to start educational or new ventures.

Amrit Choghadiya

The Moon is considered a benign planet in Vedic astrology. Hence the time under the influence of it is considered auspicious and marked as Amrit. Amrit Choghadiya is considered good for all types of work.

Kala Choghadiya

Saturn is considered a malefic planet in Vedic astrology. Hence the time under the influence of it is considered inauspicious and marked as Kala. No auspicious work is done during Kala Choghadiya. However, Kala Choghadiya is recommended for wealth related activities.

Shubh Choghadiya

Jupiter is considered a benign planet in Vedic astrology. Hence the time under the influence of it is considered auspicious and marked as Shubh. Shubh Choghadiya is considered good to conduct ceremonies especially marriage ceremonies and religious ceremonies.

Rog Choghadiya

Mars is considered a malefic planet in Vedic astrology. Hence the time under the influence of it is considered inauspicious and marked as Rog. No auspicious work is done during Rog Choghadiya. However, Rog Choghadiya is recommended for war and to defeat the enemy.

There are several apps and websites available that calculate these Muhurats based on where you are located and how the sun rises and sets in that location—just Google Choghadiya.

8

Vastu

Vastu shastra (vāstu śāstra) is a traditional Indian system of architecture that incorporates traditional Hindu beliefs and describes the principles of design, layout, measurements, ground preparation, space arrangement, and spatial geometry.

It is important to know that remedying Vastu faults in the home results in positive effects on the spiritual practices and general well being of the residents. We should locate the pooja or prayer room in the North-East corner of the house—having the pooja room in this location lets in early morning Sun's rays, which has a very beneficial effect on our health. Therefore, the North-East corner is the best position for the pooja or prayer room.

The Havan should be performed in the North-East corner of the house facing North, North-East, or East—while the God's idols or pictures should only face East or West—never South.

Pooja Room should be on the ground level, not in the basement or top floors—and never in the bedroom. It may not be possible to have a pooja room in a modern apartment—hence one can set up a small temple in the North-East corner—there should not be any toilets in that corner or even above it.

Never worship broken idols or torn pictures, such worship will bring misfortune and misery—the idols or pictures should not lean on the back wall of the temple, but should stand independently; never keep the photos of dead relatives in the pooja room or the temple.

Always use incense free from bamboo—burning bamboo is very inauspicious—always use pure ghee for lamps. Never use lighter fuel for lighting the fire in the havan, only camphor or a small cotton ball dipped in pure ghee—camphor is very convenient.

Use a woolen blanket or Kusha grass for sitting during a pooja or Havan—never sit on any wood or stone as that brings mis-fortune and misery.

9

Items Required

To perform this homam (havan) you need the following:—

1. Pictures or Idols of Gods
2. A Havan kit (kund, spoon, tongs, small bowl, glass, and plate)
3. Ghee (clarified butter)
4. Cow Dung Cakes or Mango Tree Wood
5. Dhoop or Incense (without bamboo)
6. A small Diya [lamp]
7. Sandalwood Powder
8. Tilak
9. Kalawa
10. Flowers
11. Fresh or Dry Fruits
12. Sweets (Mithai) preferably yellow or white colored
13. Some unbroken rice
14. Vegetarian Sweets [eggless] for offerings
15. Matches or Lighter
16. Camphor

17. Woolen Blanket (for sitting)
18. Drinking Water
19. Samagri (dried plants & herbs)
20. Paan - made with betel leaf, cardamom, fennel seeds, rose petal jam, clove.

Now that you have all the items, let us start performing the havan. Setup the area with setting up the idols or pictures of the Gods along with all the items, settling down on the Asana to begin.

10

Shri Vishnu Mantra

We start with a prayer to the Lord of all Universes Shri Vishnu with this mantra.

śāntākāram bhujagaśayanam padmanābham surēśam viśvādhāram
gagana-sa-dṛśam mēghavarnam śubhāṅgam lakṣmīkāntam
kamalanayanam yōgibhirdhyānagamyam vandē viṣnum
bhavabhayaharam sarvalōkaikanātham||

Meaning: Serene appearance; Resting on a bed of serpent; Lotus growing from the navel; Lord of the demigods. Beholder of the whole creation; Boundless and infinite like the sky; Bluish in color like the rainy clouds; radiating Auspiciousness.

Mahalakshmi's spouse with lotus petal like eyes; Only attainable by the Yogis and resides therein. Hail Vishnu, who banishes the fear of death; the One and the only Supreme Lord of this whole creation and all Universes.

11

Pavitrikaran Mantra

Take some water in the palm of your left hand and recite the following mantra.

om apavitraḥ pavitrō vā sarvāvasthām gatō'pi vā|
yaḥ smarētpuṇḍarīkākṣam sa bāhyā–bhyantaraḥ śuciḥ||

Meaning: Just by remembering Pundarikaksha (Lotus Eyed— one of Shri Vishnu's numerous names) one cleanses thy self both physically and mentally.

Using your ring and middle finger of your right hand, sprinkle the water from your left palm on yourself and others sitting around you while repeating Shri Vishnu's name thrice.
puṇḍarīkākṣa: punātu x 3

12

Prithvi Mantra

Recite the following mantra to sanctify the prayer and seating area.

om pṛthvi tvayā dhṛtā lōkā dēvi tvam viṣnunā dhṛtā|
tvam ca dhāraya mām dēvi pavitram kuru cāsanam||

Meaning: Om, O Goddess Prithvi (Mother Earth), You bear the whole world, and are borne by Shri Vishnu, kindly sanctify this place of worship and the seats of the worshipers.

13

Achman

Now sip a little water after reciting Lord Shri Vishnu's names.

om keśvāya namaḥ
om nārayāńa namaḥ
om mādhavāya namaḥ

With very little water, wash your hands while reciting the following.

om govindāya namaḥ

14

Ganesh Mantra

Lord Ganesh prevents any obstructions or hindrances in our pious deeds.

om vakra-ṭunndda maha-kāya ṣūrya-koṭi ṣamaprabha|
nirvighnam kuru me ḍeva sarva-kāryessu ṣarvadā ‖

Meaning: Salutations to Shri Ganesh; who has a curved trunk, who has a large body and whose splendor is similar to a million Suns; O Lord, please make my undertakings free of obstacles, by extending your blessings in all my righteous work, always.

15

Sarawati Mantra

Goddess Saraswati is the Goddess of knowledge—we pray to her for keeping our hearts and minds free of inauspicious thoughts during the havan.

om pāvakā naḥ sarasvatī vājē-bhirvāji-nīvatī|
yajñam vaṣṭu dhiyā-vasuḥ maho arnnah
sarasvatii pra cetayati ketunaa|
dhiyo vishvaa vi raajati||

Meaning: Goddess Saraswati my devotion in you increases with every ahuti (oblation).

cōdayitrī sū-nṛtānām cētantī sumatī-nām. yajñam dadhē
sarasvatī.

Meaning: Goddess Saraswati please help us hold only pure thoughts till the completion of this havan

mahō arnah sarasvatī pracēta-yeti kētunā|

dhiyō viśvā vi rājati||

Meaning: Goddess Saraswati let this Havan enlighten the entire world.

16

Gayatri Mantra

Found in the Rigveda, Gayatri mantra is one of the most important and powerful Vedic mantras and a must for every auspicious ritual.

om bhūr-bhuvaḥ svaḥ
tat-savitur-varē-nyam bhargō dēvasya dhīmahi
dhiyō yō naḥ pracō-dayāt.

Meaning: Om, neither in the Netherly plane, nor on the Earthly plane, nor in the Celestial plane — but only by meditating with dedication one finds Paramatma (The Supreme Being), resulting in complete contentment and salvation. Let us all pray to that illuminating light.

There are 14 worlds as per scriptures and they are divided in 3 parts, the Nether plane has 6 worlds, 7th being the Earthly plane, and the Celestial plane has 7 worlds.

Therefore 'Bhoor' represents the Nether planes, 'Bhuvah' represents the Earthly plane and 'Swah' represents the Celestial planes.

There is one more plane above all these, that is known as 'Vaikuntha' and that is where the 'Pramatma' resides, 'Param' means primal and 'Atma' means Soul.

17

Sankalp

'Sankalp' means pledge, now we take a pledge and declare that we are performing this Havan and name the deity and the purpose.

om mama sa kuṭumbasya sa parivārasya nitya kalyāna prāpti artham alakṣmī vināśapūrvakam aṣṭa lakṣmī prāpti artham śrī mahālakṣmī prītyartham yathā śakti śrīsūktasya hōmē viniyōgaḥ|

Meaning: I pledge that I am performing this Havan to drive away Alakshmi (misfortune); and to welcome the grace of Mahalakshmi's 8 facets into my family and clan.

You may say this is in your own words, the idea is to declare your wish that you desire from Mahalakshmi for performing this ritual.

18

Nyasa

We will perform Nyaas (activating minor chakras of our body where Goddess Mahalakshmi resides dormantly) with the following mantras.

Both hands synchronously perform the same actions. Place the tip of your index finger at the base of your thumb and slide it to the top of the thumb while chanting the following mantra.

om namō bhagavatyai mahālakṣmyai
hiranyavarnāyai aṅguṣṭhābhyām namaḥ|

Place the tip of your thumb, at the base of your index finger and slide it to the top of the index finger while chanting the following mantra.

om namō bhagavatyai mahālakṣmyai
hiranyai tarjanībhyām namaḥ|

Place the tip of your thumb, at the base of your middle finger and slide it to the top of the middle finger while chanting the following mantra.

om namō bhagavatyai mahālakṣmyai
suvarnarajatastrajāyai madhyamābhyām namaḥ|

Place the tip of your thumb, at the base of your ring finger and slide it to the top of the ring finger while chanting the following mantra.

om namō bhagavatyai mahālakṣmyai
candrāyai anāmikābhyām namaḥ|

Place the tip of your thumb, at the base of your little finger and slide it to the top of the little finger while chanting the following mantra.

om namō bhagavatyai mahālakṣmyai
hiranmayai kaniṣṭhikābhyām namaḥ|

We have to touch our imaginary 'Shikha', which is the 'tuft of hair' at the back of our head; while chanting the following mantra.

om namō bhagavatyai mahālakṣmyai
suvarna rajatastrajāyai śikhāyai namaḥ|

Now we have to bend our arms at the elbow in front of us, touching the left shoulder with your right hand and the right shoulder with your left hand to form an 'X' forming a 'Kavach' (Armour) while chanting the following mantra.

om namō bhagavatyai mahālakṣmyai
candrāyai kavacāya hum|

Gently shut your eyes and place the tip of your right hand's middle finger on the forehead between your eyebrows and place the tip of your little finger on one eye and the tip of your index finger on another eye while chanting the following mantra.

om namō bhagavatyai mahālakṣmyai
hiranmayai nētratrayāya vauṣaṭa

Now encircle your head once with your right hand while snapping your fingers and then using your middle and ring finger clap on the left palm while chanting the following mantra.

om namō bhagavatyai mahālakṣmyai astrāya phaṭa|

Now join both your hands in front of your heart, fingers facing upwards and by rotating your wrists create an imaginary circle in the air while chanting the following mantra.

om bhūrbhuvaḥ svarōmiti digbandhaḥ|

19

Mahalakshmi Invocation

Invoking the Goddess' power into our major chakras.

om arunakamal sanstha tadrāj: punjavarn,
karmal dhrteśabhitī yugamambuja ca|

Meaning: Om, Residing in the red lotus of our beautiful fingers, scaring away misery.

manimukuṭavicitrālaṅkṛtā kalpajātaiḥ
bhavatu bhuvanamātā satatam śrī śriyē naḥ|

Meaning: Adorning a crown studded with wonderful jewels, manifested to be the mother of mankind; without whom there would be no inspiration to live.

20

Offerings

After invoking the Goddess we will present our offerings—of Sandalwood Powder, Flowers, Incense, Lamp (Ghee Deepak), Un-broken Grains of Rice, and Dry Fruits (Almonds, Raisins, etc.)—if you are unable to get these items, then you must replace the words 'Samarpayami' (I offer thee physically) with the words 'Parikalpayāmi' (I offer thee spiritually)

om lam prthivyātmakan gandhan samarpayāmi|

Meaning: Om, LAM [as in lumber is the sound that activates the Muladhara (Root) Chakra] I offer thee 'Gandham' as sandalwood powder as the scent of Mother Earth.

om vam amṛtṛtatkama naivēdyam samārāpāyāmī|

Meaning: Om, VAM [as in swum is the sound that activates the Swadhisthana (Sacral) Chakra] I offer thee fruits 'Naivaidyam' the source of life *om rm tējātīkām dīpam samārāpāyāmī|*

Meaning: Om, RUM [is the sound that activates the Manipura (Solar Plexus) Chakra] I offer thee 'Tējātmakam' the radiance of life as 'dipam' lamp.

om yam vāyvātmakam dhūpan samarapayāmī|

Meaning: Om, YAM [as in yum is the sound that activates the Anahata (Heart) Chakra] I offer thee 'Vāyvātmakam' the life force as incense.

om ham ākāśātmakan puśpam samarpayāmi|

Meaning: Om, HUM [as in humming is the sound that activates the Visudhudh (Throat) Chakra] I offer thee 'Ākāśātmakam' the ether as flowers

om śam sōmatim tāmbūlādi sarvōpacārāna samarapayāmī|

Meaning: Om, ŚAM [as in Shmaltziest is the sound that activates the Ajna (Third Eye) Chakra] I offer thee 'Tāmbūlādi' the eternal youth as rice.

om chhatrm cāmaram mukuṭa pādukē samarapāyāmī (or parikalpāyāmī)|

Meaning: Om, Chattra (umbrella), Chamram (cowrie), Mukut (daidem), Paduka (sandals) I offer thee. Remember if these objects are not physically present for offering then replace the words 'samarapayami' with 'parikalpayami', which means that you are offering them spiritually.

21

Agni Mantra

We will light the fire in the Havan kund, you can use the camphor to start the fire

om agnimīlē purōhitm yajñasya dēvamṛtvijam|
hotarum ratnadhātam||

Meaning: Om, O Agni Dev, we are grateful to you for transporting our ahutis (oblations) to our deity through this havan.

22

Shri Suktam

Now we will begin the main mantras of Shri Suktam to please the Goddess of Wealth and Prosperity—pour a spoon of Ghee after every verse.

There were 15 verses in the original Shri Suktam, more were added by the great sages and seers over the last 5,000 years—bringing the total to 37 verses.

You must pour the oblations only after reciting each verse of Shri Suktam—remember to say "Swāhā" and pour a spoon of ghee into the Havan kund as oblation.

Since there are 37 ahutis (oblations) required—one for every verse, but you should take about 45 spoons of Ghee, it is always better to have some extra ghee that will keep the fire going for Shanti Mantras.

Ideally we must keep the fire burning until the completion of Shanti mantras which come after Shri Suktam, you can always throw in a small piece of camphor if the flame gets dim or to rekindle the fire.

The Havan kund's fire must be shielded from strong wind, because it is inauspicious if the fire extinguishes during the Havan, switch off the fan, but remember to have good ventilation in the room where you are performing the havan.

If there is too much smoke in the havan kund, then the fire is gasping for air and needs to breath, adjust the cow dung cakes to let in some air, if the flame is too dim, then it needs more ghee—it takes some practice to get it right and you will be able to find the balance after a few tries.

So let's begin this miraculous ritual.

harih om
hiranya-varnām harinīm suvarna-rajatasra-jām|
candrām hiranmayī lakṣmīm jātavēdō ma āvaha||1||
"Swāhā"

Meaning: Harih Om (Salutations for Lord Shri Vishnu) The one who is agile like a deer, shimmers like gold with a greenish aura. Adorning necklaces made of gold and silver. O Fire God, Please bring the grace of that Mahalakshmi for me||1||

tām ma āvaha jātavēdō lakṣmīm-anapagāminīm|
yasyām hiranyam vindēyam gāmaśvam puruṣānaham||2||
"Swāhā"

Meaning: O Fire God, bring the undiminishing grace of Mahalakshmi, allowing my descendants and me, to gain employees and associates who will help us (generate wealth) by raising cattle and horses||2||

aśva-purvanam ratha-madhyām ḥastinād prabodhinim|
śriyam dēvī-mupahvayē śrīrmā dēvī juṣatām||3||
"Swāhā"

Meaning: Like a victory parade, let Mahalakshmi's grace (prosperity) come marching into my life riding on a chariot drawn by horses—amidst the roaring trumpets of elephants||3||

kām sōsmitām hiranya-prākārām-ārdrām
jvalantīm tṛptām tarpayantīm|
padmē sthitām padmavarnan
tamihō-pahvaya śriyam||4||
"Swāhā"

Meaning: So that all my wishes are fulfilled, bring me the grace of the ever smiling and glowing like gold Mahalakshmi, who sits on the lotus with a heart as soft||4||

candrām prabhāsām yaśasā jvalantīm
śriyam lōkē dēvajuṣṭāmudārām|
tām padminīmīn śaranamham prapadye
alakśmīrme naśyatām tvām vṛune||5||
"Swāhā"

Meaning: Your divinity shines like moonlight upon all worlds, revered alike by Gods, Demigods, and all beings. I am in your refuge, please rid Alakshmi (misfortune) from my life||5||

ādityavarnē tapasō'dhijātō vanaspatistava vṛkṣō'tha bilvaḥ|
tasya phlāni tapasanudantu mayān-tarāyanāśca bāhya
alakṣmiḥ||6||
"Swāhā"

Meaning: You generated the "wood apple" (Bilva) tree with the magnanimity of your divine prowess—using the same magnanimity, please raise me up from the illusions of this material world and misfortune||6||

upaitu mām dēvasakhaḥ kīrtiśca maninā saha|
pradur-bhutō'smi rāstrē'smin kirtimrudhim dhadhātu mē||7||
"Swāhā"

Meaning: Grant me a 'Mani' (a jewel that generates gold), similar to which Kubera (treasurer of Gods) possesses and 'Kirti' (fame). So that I can be as rich and famous as him||7||

kśutpi-pāsāmalām jyeśthām-alakśmī nāśayāmyaham|
ābhūtimā-samrddhim ca ṣarvām nirnnu-da me gruhāt||8||
"Swāhā"

Meaning: Let there never be dearth of food or water in my home, guard us from your elder sister Alakshmi (misfortune)||8||

gandhadvāram durādharśam nityapuśtam karīśinīm|
īśvarīng sarvabhūtānām tāmihopahvaye śriyam||9||
"Swāhā"

Meaning: Like the odor of smeared cow dung keeps the diseases away from one's home—may the fragrance of your grace, keep anguish away from my household||9||

manasaḥ kāmamā-kootim vācaḥ satya-maśīmahi|
paśūnām rūpa-mannasya mayi śrīḥ śrayatām yaśaḥ||10||
"Swāhā"

Meaning: Just as various sweets can be made from milk, guide my intellect to generate beneficial ideas and complete virtuous projects that glorify your grace||10||

kardamena praja-bhūta mayi sambhav kardāma|
śriyam vāsaya me kule mātaram padmamālinīm||11||
"Swāhā"

Meaning: O Padmamalini [one who wears the garland of Lotus], heed my prayer as you would of your son Kardam. Forever grace my clan with your presence||11||

āapah ṣrjantu ṣnigdhāni chiklīta vasa me gruhe|
ni cha ḍevī mātaram ṣriyam vāsaya me kule||12||
"Swāhā"

Meaning: As rain quenches parched cracked ground, forever shower my clan with your grace||12||

āardrām pusskarinnī pussttim pinggalām padma-mālinīm|
chandrām ḥirannmayī lakssmī jātavedo ma āavaha||13||
"Swāhā"

Meaning: Agni Dev (Fire God), Bring showers of grace of that Mahalakshmi, who glows like moonlight, to fill my life like a pond of blessed blooming lotuses||13||

āardrām yaḥ karinnīm yassttim ṣuvarnnām ḥema-mālinīm|
ṣūryām ḥirannmayīm lakssmīm jātavedo ma āavaha||14||
"Swāhā"

Meaning: O Fire God, So that these ponds always remain full with the blessed golden lotuses, bring the grace of that Mahalakshmi, who shimmers like the Sun||14||

tām ma āavaha jātavedo lakssmīm-anapagāminīm|
yasyām ḥirannyam prabhūtam gāvo dāsyo-śvān vindeyam
pūrussānaham||15||
"Swāhā"

Meaning: Agni Dev (Fire God),
   Bring Mahalakshmi's undiminishable grace that grants riches in the form of cattle, horses, and progeny to complete my virtuous pursuits||15||

yah ṣucih prayato bhūtvā juhu-yād-jyaman-vaham|
ṣūktam pancā-daśarcan ca śrīkāmaḥ ṣatatam japet||16||
"Swāhā"

Meaning: Let my deeds always be as virtuous and as sacred and pure as the oblations of the ghee that I pour in this Shri Suktam ritual||16||

padmanane padma ūrū padmākśī padmāsambhave|
tvam mām bhajasv padmākśī yen saukhyam labhāmyaham||17||
"Swāhā"

Meaning: Beautiful as the lotus, sitting on the laps of lotus petals, lotus eyed, manifested holding a lotus—success comes easily to those who worship you||17||

aśva-ḍāyi go-ḍāyi dhana-dāyi mahā-dhane|
dhanam me jussatām ḍevi ṣarva-kāmāmś-cā ḍehi me||18||
"Swāhā"

Meaning: Your worshippers are blessed with cattle, horses, and great riches, Dear Goddess—do fulfill all my virtuous desires and goals||18||

putra-pautra dhanam dhānyam hastyaśvādigave ratham|
prajānām bhavasi mātā āayussmantam karo-tu mām||19||
"Swāhā"

Meaning: Bless me with sons, grandsons, wealth, grains, elephants, horses, chariots, and a healthy long life to enjoy your blessings||19||

dhanam-āgnir-dhanam vāyur-dhanam ṣūryo dhanam vasuḥ|
dhanam-īndro brhaspatir-varunnam dhanam-āśnute||20||
"Swāhā"

Meaning: You are the heat in the fire, the life force in the air, the radiance in the sun, the intelligence in Indra [King of Demigods], the knowledge in Brihaspati (Demigod's Guru) and the currents in the oceans||20||

vainateya ṣomam piba ṣomam pibatu vrtrahā|
ṣomam dhanasya ṣomino mahyam ḍadātu ṣominaḥ||21||

"Swāhā"

Meaning: You let Vinata's son Garud (Falcon - Lord Vishnu's ride) drink 'Som Ras' (elixir of life to defeat demons). Grant me the same, making me invincible||21||

na krodho na ca mātsarya na lobho na-āśubhā matih|
bhavanti krutapunnyānām bhaktānām śrīsūktam japet-sadā||22||
"Swāhā"

Meaning: Regularly performing, Shri Suktam's havan, liberates one from anger, jealousy, greed, and inauspicious thoughts||22||

varśantu te vibhāvari divo ābhrasya vidyutah|
rohantu sarva-bīja-ānyava brahma dviṣo jahi||23||
"Swāhā"

Meaning: Your re-emergence (from ocean churning), like a bolt of lightning, cleared the dark clouds of war between Demigods and Asuras—thus saving the universe from total annihilation||23||

padmapriye padmini padmahaste padmālaye padmadalāyatākśi|
viśvapriye viśnu manonukūle tvatpādapadmam mayi
sannidhatsva||24||
"Swāhā"

Meaning: Padmapriya Padmini, holding a lotus, wearing a lotus garland, lotus eyed—revered universally, Vishnu's most adored—grant me refuge in your lotus feet||24||

ya sa padma-sanasthā vipula-kaṭitaṭi padma-patrāya-tākśī|
gambhīra vartanābhih stanabhar namita śubhra vastrutriyā||25||
"Swāhā"

Meaning: O Lotus petal eyed, beautifully dressed Goddess—
Shield me from all harm (in this life and afterlife) like a caring
mother who nourishes her baby through the umbilical cord
in her womb, and after birth keeps her child close to her
bosom||25||

lakśmīr-divyair-gajendrair-mani-gana-khacittay-snāpita-
hema-kumbhaih|
nityan sa padmahasta mam vasatu gruhe
sarvamāngalya-yukta||26||
"Swāhā"

Meaning: Padmahasta (lotus bearer) — O lotus holding Goddess,
please grace my house with your eternal presence so that
even I may regularly bathe your feet with the 'Mani' studded
golden ornamental pitcher—as Gajendra (the king of elephants)
does||26||

lakśmīm kśīr-samudra rāja-tanayam śrīranga-dhāmeśvarīm|
dāsī-būtha-samasta dev vanitām lokaika dīpānkurām||27||
"Swāhā"

Meaning: O Princess of the oceans, your re-emergence (from
ocean churning) brought back the light of 'Shri' (auspiciousness) into this universe, for which all living beings are eternally
indebted to you||27||

śrīman-manda-katākś-labdha vibhav
brahmendra-gangādharām|
tvām trai-lokya kutum-binīm sara-sijām vande
mukunda-priyām||28||
"Swāhā"

Meaning: Mukundpriya (Lord Shri Vishnu's beloved) all the beings of the tri-worlds is your family, Brahma, Indra, and Gangadhar (Lord Shiva) were glorified when you gazed upon them||28||

siddha-lakśmīr-mokśa-lakśmīr-jayalakśmī-sarasvatī|
srilakśmīr-varalakśmīś-cā prasanna mam sarvadā||29||
"Swāhā"

Meaning: Granter of Siddhi, Moksh, Success, Knowledge, Grandeur, and Wishes; remain pleased with me forever||29||

varān-kuśau pāśam-bhīti-mudram
karair-vahantim kamalā-sanasthām|
bālārk koṭi pratibhām trinritam bhajeha-mādyam
jagadīsvarīm tvām||30||
"Swāhā"

Meaning: Four armed Jagadishwari, your tri-eyed form is as brilliant as a million sunrises—you hold a prod in one hand, a noose in the second, abhay (fearless) mudra in the third and boons flow from your fourth hand||30||

sarva-mangala-māngalye śive sarvārth sādhike|
śaranye tryambake devi nārāyanī namos-tu-te nārāyanī

namos-tu-te nārāyanī namos-tu-te||31||
"Swāhā"

Meaning: Tri-eyed you are always propitious to your seekers, I seek your refuge. Narayani (Vishnu's Wife), reverential salutations to you; Narayani, reverential salutations to you; Narayani, reverential salutations to you||31||

sarasija-nilaye saroja-haste dhavala-tarānśuk
gandha-mālya-śobhe|
bhagavatī hari-vallabhe mañogye
tribhuvana-bhootikarī prasīd mahyam||32||
"Swāhā"

Meaning: One who resides in a lotus, always holds a lotus, dressed ornately, wearing fragrant garlands—Bhagwati, adored by Vishnu—you are the source of all happiness in all three realms (Physical, Mental and Spiritual)||32||

viśnu-patnī kśamām devī mādhvi mādhav-priyām|
viśnoh priya-sakhī devi na-māmya-acyuta-vallabham||33||
"Swāhā"

Meaning: Vishnu's wife, the most forgiving Goddess, Madhavi (Vishnu's wife), Madhav's (Vishnu's) beloved Vishnu's soulmate, Achyut's (Vishnu's) most adored Goddess I offer my humble obeisances||33||

mahālakśmī ca vidmahe viśnu-patnī ca dhīmahi|
tanno lakśmīḥ pracho-dayāt||34||
"Swāhā"

Meaning: Mahalakshmi, Vishnu's wife, dedicatedly worshiping you inspires us (to do good) and strengthens our faith||34||

śrī-varchasya-māyuśya-mārogya-māvidhāt pavamānam
mahiyate|
dhanam dhānyam paśu bahu-putra-lābham
śata-smvatsaram dīrgham-āyuḥ||35||
"Swaha"

Meaning: To fully enjoy your bestowed blessings of Sons, Wealth, Granaries, and Cattle, grant me a healthy long life of a century||35||

r̥inarogā-didāridrya-pāp-akśudapa-mrtyavaḥ|
bhaya-śoka-manastāpa naśyantu mam sarvada||36||
"Swāhā"

Meaning: Grant me a life free of debt, disease, poverty, sin, famine, accidental death, fear, grief, and anguish||36||

ya evam ved|
om mahādaivyai ca vidmahe viśnu-patnī ca dhīmahi|
tanno lakśmīḥ pracodayāt||37||
"Swāhā"

om shāntiḥ shāntiḥ shāntiḥ

Meaning: That's the ultimate truth! O great Goddess—Vishnu's wife. We all bow to you with inspiration & loyalty.
Om Peace, Peace, Peace||37||

Shri Suktam is now complete; however, to conclude the Havan we must recite the Purnahuti and Shanti Mantra for peace and prosperity of every living being in this universe—whether movable or immovable.

23

Purnahuti Mantra

While reciting the following mantra, you must slowly pour the remaining ghee & samagri into the Havan kund, taking care not to extinguish the flame or causing conflagration.

om pūrna-madaḥ pūrna-midam pūrnāt-pūrna-mudacyate|
pūrnasy pūrna-mādāy pūrna-mevā-vaśiśyate||
om shāntiḥ shāntiḥ shāntiḥ||

Meaning: Om, A Divine Consciousness (Life Force) exists in this whole creation, the same resides within and without every being - it remains constant, even if it manifests into many forms, it never decimates.

Om Peace, Peace, Peace

24

Shanti Mantra

These are the final mantras that will conclude our havan.

om bhadram karnnebhih ṣrnnuyāma ḍevāḥ|
bhadram paśyemā–kśabhirya–jatrāh|
ṣthirair–rānggais–ṭuśttuvāgamsas–tanūbhiḥ|
vyaśema ḍevaḥi–tam yadā–yuḥ|

Meaning: O God, May our ears always hear your auspicious name. May our eyes always see your auspicious image. May our faith in you remain steady and your praises remain on our lips till the end of days.

svāsti na indrō vṛd'dhā āśravaḥ|
svāstī ēna: puśā viśvavēdaḥ|
svāstī nastarakṣyō ariṣṭanēmīḥ|
svāsti nō bhrshaspatir–datātu||
om shāntiḥ shāntiḥ shāntiḥ||

Meaning: Grant us Wisdom from Indra (King of Demigods),

Knowledge from Sun (Knower of all Vedas), unstoppable God-speed from Tarksyu (Garud's elder brother), and Guidance from Brihaspati (Guru of the Demigods)
Om Peace, Peace, Peace

om dyauḥ śāntirantarikṣaṁ śāntiḥ
pṛthivī śāntirāpaḥ śāntirōṣadhayaḥ śāntiḥ|
vanaspatayaḥ śāntirviśvēdēvāḥ śāntirbrahma śāntiḥ
sarvaṁ śāntiḥ śāntirēva śāntiḥ sā mā śāntirēdhi||
om śāntiḥ śāntiḥ śāntiḥ||

Meaning: Om, Peace in heaven, peace in space, peace on earth; Peace in water; Peace in plants; Peace in trees; Peace in the gods; Peace in the universe; Peace in all; Peace within me; Peace within you;

Om Peace Peace Peace

25

Kshama Yachana

Mother Mahalakshmi, your Havan is now complete, kindly forgive us for any errors or lapses that we might have committed while performing this sacred havan. Always keep us in your good graces!

26

After The Havan

Do not extinguish the flame, let it cool down on its own; the ashes are sacred, so don't throw them in a dustbin, you may use the ash as a fertilizer in your garden or scatter it in any clean river, lake or sea.

Always have multiple copies of this booklet in your home, so that you can gift it to your family and friends, enabling them to also perform this miraculous Havan in their own homes and generate additional grace for you.

27

Pushpabhishek

'Pushp' means flowers and 'Abhishek' means showering or bathing.

In Shri Suktam Havan there are many mantras and it takes about half an hour to complete and requires a lot of items, but Pushpabhishek can be done with fewer items like: Flowers, incense, lamp, drinking water and fresh or dry fruits.

There are only 16 verses in Shri Suktam Pushpabhishek and can be completed in about 15 minutes and easy enough to be done daily.

A complete audio and video with the mantras is part of the DLC.

Shri Vishnu Mantra

śāntākāram bhujagaśayanam padmanābham surēśam viśvādhāram gaganasadṛśam

mēghavarnam śubhāṅgam. lakṣmīkāntam kamalanayanam yōgibhirdhyānagamyam vandē viśhnu bhavabhayaharam sarvalōkaikanātham||

Pavitrikaran Mantra

om apavitraḥ pavitrō vā sarvāvasthām gatōpi vā|
yaḥ smarētpuṇḍarīkākṣam sa bāhyābhyantaraḥ śuciḥ||

Prithvi Mantra

om pṛthvi tvayā dhṛtā lōkā dēvi tvam viṣnunā dhṛtā| tvam ca
dhāraya mām dēvi
pavitram kuru cāsanam||

Achman

om keśvāya namaḥ
om nārayāńa namaḥ
om mādhavāya nama

Hastaprakshalay

om govindāya namaḥ

Ganesh Mantra

om vakra-tunndda maha-kāya ṣūrya-koṭi ṣamaprabha|
nirvighnam kuru me ḍeva sarva-kāryessu ṣarvadā ||

Gayatri Mantra

om bhūrbhuvaḥ svaḥ tatsaviturvarēnyam bhargō
dēvasya dhīmahi dhiyō yō naḥ pracōdayāt.

Sankalp (Declaration)

om mama sa kuṭumbasya sa parivārasya nitya kalyāna prāpti
artham alakṣmī

vināśapūrvakam aṣṭa lakṣmī prāpti artham śrī mahālakṣmī prītyartham yathā śakti

śrīsūktasya hōmē viniyōgaḥ|

Mahalakshmi Invocation

om arunakamal sanstha tadrāj: punjavarn, karmal dhruteśa-bhitī yugama-ambuja ca|

mani-mukuṭa-vicitrā-laṅkṛtā kalpajātaiḥ bhavatu bhu-vanamātā satatam śrī śriyē

naḥ||

Offerings

om lam prthivyātmakan gandhan samarpayāmi|

om vam amṛtṛtatkama naivēdyam samārāpāyāmī|

om rm tējātīkām dīpam samārāpāyāmī|

om yam vāyvātmakam dhūpan samarapayāmī|

om ham ākāśātmakan puśpam samarpayāmi|

om śam sōmatim tāmbūlādi sarvōpacārāna samarapayāmī|

om chhtram cāmaram mukuṭa pādukē samarapāyāmī|

Shri Suktam

hariḥ om

hiranya-varnām harinīm suvarna-rajatasra-jām| candrām hiranmayī lakṣmīm

jātavēdō ma āvaha||1||

tām ma āvaha jātavēdō lakṣmīm-anapagāminīm| yasyām hiranyam vindēyam

gāmaśvam-puruṣānaham||2||

aśva-purvanam ratha-madhyām hastinād prabodhinim|

śriyam dēvī-mupahvayē śrīrmā dēvī juṣatām||3||

kām sōsmitām hiranyaprākārāmārdrām jvalantīm tṛptām

tarpayantīm|
    padmē sthitām padmavarnan tamihōpahvaya śriyam||4||
    candrām prabhāsām yaśasā jvalantīm śriyam lōkē dēvajuṣṭā-
mudārām|
    tām padminīmīn śaranamham prapadye alakśmīrme||5||
    ādityavarnē tapasō'dhijātō vanaspatistava vṛkṣō'tha bilvaḥ|
    tasya phlāni tapasanudantu manturanāśca bāhya alakṣmiḥ||6||
    upaitu mām dēvasakhaḥ kīrtiśca maninā saha|
    pradurbhutō'smi rāstrē'smin kirtimrudhim dhadhātu mē||7||
    kśutpi-pāsāmalām jyeśthām-alakśmī nāśayāmyaham|
    ābhūtimā-samrddhim cha ṣarvām nirnnuda me gruhāt||8||
    gandhad-vāram durā-dharśam nitya-puśtam karī-śinīm|
    īśvarīng sarva-bhūtānām tāmiho-pahvaye śriyam||9||
    manasaḥ kāmamā-kuntim vācaḥ satya-maśīmahi|
    paśūnām rūpa-mannasya mayi śrīḥ śrayatām yaśaḥ||10||
    karnmena praja-bhūta mayi sambhav kardāma| śriyam
vāsaya me kule mātaram
    padmamālinīm||11||
    āapah śrjantu ṣnigdhāni chiklīta vasa me gruhe|
    ni cha ḍevī mātaram ṣriyam vāsaya me kule||12||
    āardrām pusskarinnī pussttim pinggalām padma-mālinīm|
    chandrām ḥirannmayī lakssmī ātavedo ma āavaha||13||
    āardrām yaḥ karinnīm yassttim ṣuvarnnām ḥema-mālinīm|
ṣūryām ḥirannmayīm
    lakssmīm jātavedo ma āavaha||14||
    tām ma āavaha jātavedo lakssmīm-anapagāminīm|
    yasyām ḥirannyam prabhūtam gāvo dāsyo-śvān vindeyam
pūrussānaham||15||
    yah ṣucih prayato bhūtvā juhu-yād-jyaman-vaham|
    ṣūktam panadaśarcam cha ṣrīkāmaḥ ṣatatam japet||16||

Kshama Yachana

Mother Mahalakshmi, your Havan is now complete, kindly forgive us for any errors or

lapses that we might have committed while performing this sacred havan.

Always keep us in your good graces!

This concludes the Pushpabhishek

28

All Mantras

Shri Vishnu Mantra

śāntākāram bhujagaśayanam padmanābham surēśam viśvādhāram gaganasadṛśam

mēghavarnam śubhāṅgam. lakṣmīkāntam kamalanayanam
yōgibhirdhyānagamyam

vandē viśhnu bhavabhayaharam sarvalōkaikanātham||

Pavitrikaran Mantra

om apavitraḥ pavitrō vā sarvāvasthām gatōpi vā|
yaḥ smarētpuṇḍarīkākṣam sa bāhyābhyantaraḥ śuciḥ||

Prithvi Mantra

om pṛthvi tvayā dhṛtā lōkā dēvi tvam viṣnunā dhṛtā| tvam ca
dhāraya mām dēvi

pavitram kuru cāsanam||

Achman

om keśvāya namaḥ
om nārayāńa namaḥ

om mādhavāya nama

Hastaprakshalay

om govindāya namaḥ

Ganesh Mantra

om vakra-tunndda maha-kāya ṣūrya-koṭi ṣamaprabha|
nirvighnam kuru me ḍeva
sarva-kāryessu ṣarvadā ॥

Saraswati Mantra

om pāvakā naḥ sarasvatī vājēbhirvājinīvatī| yajñam vaṣṭu
dhiyāvasuḥ maho arnnah
sarasvatii pra cetayati ketunaa| dhiyo vishvaa vi raajati||
cōdayitrī sūnṛtānām cētantī sumatīnām|
yajñam dadhē sarasvatī.
mahō arnaḥ sarasvatī pra cētayati kētunā|
viśvā vi rājat ॥

Gayatri Mantra

om bhūrbhuvaḥ svaḥ tatsaviturvarēnyam bhargō dēvasya
dhīmahi dhiyō yō naḥ
pracōdayāt.

Sankalp (Declaration)

om mama sa kuṭumbasya sa parivārasya nitya kalyāna prāpti
artham alakṣmī
vināśapūrvakam aṣṭa lakṣmī prāpti artham śrī mahālakṣmī
prītyartham yathā śakti
śrīsūktasya hōmē viniyōgaḥ|

Nyaas

om namō bhagavatyai mahālakṣmyai hiranyavarnāyai aṅguṣṭhābhyām namaḥ|

om namō bhagavatyai mahālakṣmyai hiranyai tarjanībhyām namaḥ|

om namō bhagavatyai mahālakṣmyai suvarnarajatastrajāyai madhyamābhyām

namaḥ|

om namō bhagavatyai mahālakṣmyai candrāyai anāmikābhyām namaḥ|

om namō bhagavatyai mahālakṣmyai hiranmayai kaniṣṭhikābhyām namaḥ|

om namō bhagavatyai mahālakṣmyai suvarna rajatastrajāyai śikhāyai namaḥ|

om namō bhagavatyai mahālakṣmyai candrāyai kavacāya hum|

om namō bhagavatyai mahālakṣmyai candrāyai kavacāya hum|

om namō bhagavatyai mahālakṣmyai hiranmayai nētratrayāya vauṣaṭa|

om namō bhagavatyai mahālakṣmyai astrāya phaṭa|

om bhūrbhuvaḥ svarōmiti digbandhaḥ|

Mahalakshmi Invocation

om arunakamal sanstha tadrāj: punjavarn, karmal dhruteśabhitī yugama–ambuja ca|

mani-mukuṭa-vicitrā-laṅkṛtā kalpajātaiḥ bhavatu bhuvanamātā satatam śrī śriyē

naḥ||

Offerings

om lam prthivyātmakan gandhan samarpayāmi|
om vam amṛtṛtatkama naivēdyam samārāpāyāmī|
om rm tējātīkām dīpam samārāpāyāmī|
om yam vāyvātmakam dhūpan samarapayāmī|
om ham ākāśātmakan puśpam samarpayāmi|
om śam sōmatim tāmbūlādi sarvōpacārāna samarapayāmī|
om chhtram cāmaram mukuṭa pādukē samarapāyāmī|

Agni Mantra

om agnimīlē purōhitm yajñasya dēvamṛtvijam| hotarum rat-
nadhātam||

Shri Suktam

hariḥ om
hiranya-varnām harinīm suvarna-rajatasra-jām| candrām
hiranmayī lakṣmīm
jātavēdō ma āvaha||1||
tām ma āvaha jātavēdō lakṣmīm-anapagāminīm| yasyām
hiranyam vindēyam
gāmaśvam-puruṣānaham||2||
aśva-purvanam ratha-madhyām ḥastinād prabodhinim|
śriyam dēvī-mupahvayē
śrīrmā dēvī juṣatām||3||
kām sōsmitām hiranyaprākārāmārdrām jvalantīm tṛptām
tarpayantīm| padmē
sthitām padmavarnan tamihōpahvaya śriyam||4||
candrām prabhāsām yaśasā jvalantīm śriyam lōkē dēvajuṣṭā-
mudārām| tām
padminīmīn śaranamham prapadye alakśmīrme||5||
ādityavarnē tapasō'dhijātō vanaspatistava vṛkṣō'tha bilvaḥ|
tasya phlāni tapasanudantu

manturanāśca bāhya alakṣmiḥ||6||

upaitu mām dēvasakhaḥ kīrtiśca maninā saha| pradurb-hutō'smi rāstrē'smin

kirtimrudhim

dhadhātu mē||7||

kśutpi-pāsāmalām jyeśthām-alakśmī nāśayāmyaham|

ābhūtimā-samrddhim cha ṣarvām nirnnuda me gruhāt||8||

gandhad-vāram durā-dharśam nitya-puśtam karī-śinīm|

īśvarīng sarva-bhūtānām

tāmiho-pahvaye śriyam||9||

manasaḥ kāmamā-kuntim vācaḥ satya-maśīmahi| paśūnām

rūpa-mannasya mayi

śrīḥ śrayatām yaśaḥ||10||

karnmena praja-bhūta mayi sambhav kardāma| śriyam

vāsaya me kule mātaram

padmamālinīm||11||

āapah śrjantu ṣnigdhāni chiklīta vasa me gruhe| ni cha ḍevī

mātaram ṣriyam vāsaya

me kule||12||

āardrām pusskarinnī pussttim pinggalām padma-mālinīm|

chandrām hirannmayī

lakssmī ātavedo ma āavaha||13||

āardrām yaḥ karinnīm yassttim ṣuvarnnām hema-mālinīm|

ṣūryām hirannmayīm

lakssmīm jātavedo ma āavaha||14||

tām ma āavaha jātavedo lakssmīm-anapagāminīm| yasyām

hirannyam prabhūtam

gāvo dāsyo-śvān vindeyam pūrussānaham||15||

yah ṣucih prayato bhūtvā juhu-yād-jyaman-vaham| ṣūktam

panadaśarcam cha

ṣrīkāmaḥ ṣatatam japet||16||

padmanane padma ūrū padmākṣī padmāsambhave|
tvam mām bhajasv padmākṣī yen saukhyam labhāmya-
ham||17||
aśva-ḍāyi go-ḍāyi dhana-dāyi mahā-dhane|
dhanam me jussatām ḍevi ṣarva-kāmāmś-cha ḍehi me||18||
putra-pautra dhanam dhānyam hastyaśvādigave ratham|
prajānām bhavasi mātā
āayussmantam karotu mām||19||
dhanam-āgnir-dhanam vāyur-dhanam ṣūryo dhanam vasuḥ|
dhanam-īndro
brhaspatir-varunnam dhanam-āśnute||20||
vainateya ṣomam piba ṣomam pibatu vrtrahā| ṣomam
dhanasya ṣomino mahyam
ḍadātu ṣominaḥ||21||
na krodho na cha mātsarya na lobho na-āśubhā matih| bha-
vanti krutapunnyānām
bhaktānām śrīsūktam japet-sadā||22||
varssantu te vibhāvari divo ābhrasya vidyutah| rohantu sarva-
bīja-ānyava brahma
ḍviṣo jahi||23||
padmapriye padmini padmahaste padmālaye padmadalāy-
atākśi| viśvapriye viṣnu
manonukūle tvatpādapadmam mayi sannidhatsva||24||
ya sa padmasanasthā vipulakaṭitaṭi padmapatrāyatākśī|
gambhīra vartanābhih
stanabhar namita śubhra vastrutriyā||25||
lakśmīr-divyair-gajendrair-mani-gana-khacittas-snāpita
hema-kumbhaih| nityan
sa padmahasta mam vasatu gruhe sarvamāngalya-yukta||26||
lakśmīm kśīraj-samudra rāja-tanayam śrīranga-dhāmeśvarīm|
dāsī-būthasamasta

dev vanitām lokaika dīpānkurām||27||

śriman-mandakatākś-labdha vibhav brahmendra-gangādharām|
tavam trai-lokya

kutum-binīm sara-sijām vande mukunda-priyām||28||

siddha-lakśmīr-mokśa-lakśmīr-jayalakśmī-sarasvatī|
śrilakśmīr-varalakśmīś-ca

prasanna mam

sarvada||29||

varān-kuśau pāśam-bhīti-mudram karair-vahantim kamalā-
sanasthām| bālārk koti

pratibhām trinritam bhajeha-mādyam jagadīsvarīm tvām||30||

sarva-mangala-māngalye śive sarvārth sādhike|

śaranye tryambake devi nārāyanī namos-tu-te

nārāyanī namos-tu-te nārāyanī namos-tu-te||31||

sarasija-nilaye saroja-haste dhavala-tarānśuk gandha-
mālya-śobhe| bhagavatī hari

vallabhe mañogye tribhuvana-bhootikarī prasīd mahyam||32||

viśnu-patnī kśamām devī mādhvi mādhav-priyām| viśnoh
priya-sakhī devi

namāmya-acyuta-vallabham||33||

mahālakśmī ca vidmahe viśnu-patnī ca dhīmahi| tanno
lakśmīḥ pracho-dayāt||34||

śrī-varchasya-māyuśya-mārogya-māvidhāt pavamānam
mahiyate| dhanam

dhānyam paśu bahu-putra-lābham śata-smvatsaram
dīrgham-āyuḥ||35||

ṛinarogā-didāridrya-pāp-akśudapa-mrtyavaḥ|

bhaya-śoka-manastāpa naśyantu mam sarvada||36||

ya evam ved|

om mahādaivyai ca vidmahe viśnu-patnī ca dhīmahi| tanno
lakśmīḥ pracodayāt||37||

om shāntiḥ shāntiḥ shāntiḥ

Purnahuti Mantra

om pūrna-madaḥ pūrna-midam pūrnāt-pūrna-mudacyate|
pūrnasy pūrna-mādāy
pūrna-mevā-vaśiśyate||
om shāntiḥ shāntiḥ shāntiḥ||

Shanti Mantra

om bhadram karnnebhih ṣrnnuyāma ḍevāḥ| bhadram
paśyemā-kśabhirya-jatrāh|
ṣthirair-rānggais-ṭuśttuvāgamsas-tanūbhiḥ| vyaśema
ḍevaḥi-tam yadā-yuḥ|
svāsti na indrō vṛd'dhā āśravaḥ| svāstī ēna: puśā viśvavēdaḥ
svāstī nastarakṣyō
ariṣṭanēmīḥ| svāsti nō bhrshaspatir-datātu.||
om shāntiḥ shāntiḥ shāntiḥ||
om dyauḥ śāntirantarikṣaṁ śāntiḥ
pṛthivī śāntirāpaḥ śāntirōṣadhayaḥ śāntiḥ|
vanaspatayaḥ śāntirviśvēdēvāḥ śāntirbrahma śāntiḥ
sarvaṁ śāntiḥ śāntirēva śāntiḥ sā mā śāntirēdhi||
om śāntiḥ śāntiḥ śāntiḥ||

29

Downloadable Content

We understand that the mantras presented in this book can be challenging to pronounce, especially for those new to Sanskrit or unfamiliar with Vedic chanting. To address this common issue and enhance your learning experience, we've taken several steps to make these sacred sounds more accessible:

1. Professional Audio Recording: We've enlisted the expertise of a highly trained, professional Sanskrit singer to record each mantra with precise pronunciation. This ensures that you can hear the correct intonation, rhythm, and emphasis for every syllable.
2. Instructional Video Content: In addition to the audio recordings, we've produced high-quality video content to aid in your learning process. These videos provide:

Visual representations of the Sanskrit text
   - Phonetic breakdowns of each mantra
   - Slow, step-by-step pronunciation guides
   - Information on the meaning and significance of each mantra

To obtain these exclusive audio and video resources:

1. Locate your purchase receipt for this book.
2. Send an email to shrivandebharti@gmail.com with the subject line "Mantra Resources Request".
3. Attach a copy or clear legible photo of your purchase receipt to the email.
4. In the body of the email, please include:

- Your full name [must match the name in the invoice.
- Date of purchase

Once we verify your purchase, we'll promptly reply with detailed instructions on how to download the audio files and access the video content. Please allow up to 2-3 business days for processing.

We're committed to supporting your spiritual journey and helping you develop a deeper connection with these powerful mantras. Should you have any questions or need additional assistance, please don't hesitate to reach us at shrivandebharti @gmail.com.

Remember, consistent practice and patient persistence are key to mastering these mantras. We encourage you to make use of these resources regularly and wish you a fulfilling and transformative experience as you explore the profound wisdom contained within these sacred sounds.

***

30

Sanskrit Pronunciation Guide

The Vowels:
  a – as in but
  ā – as in far
  i – as in pin
  ī – as in pique but held twice as long as i
  u – as in push
  ū – as in rule but held twice as long as u
  r – as in rim
  e – as in they
  ai – as in aisle
  o – as in go
  au – as in how

The Consonants:
  Gutterals (pronounced from the throat)
  k – as in kite
  kh – as in Ekhart
  g – as in give
  gh – as in aghast

ṅ – as in sing
Labials (pronounced with the lips)
p – as in pine
ph – as in haphazard (not f)
b – as in bird
bh – as in abhor
m –as in mother

Cerebrals (pronounced with tongue against roof of mouth)
ṭ – as in tub
ṭh – as in light-heart
ḍ – as in dove
ḍh – as in adhere
ṅ – as in sing
Palatals (pronounced with middle of tongue against palate)
c – as in chair
ch – as in staunch-heart
j – as in joy
jh – as in hedgehog
ñ – as in canyon

Dentals (pronounced with tongue against teeth)
t – as in pasta
th – as in think
d – as in the
dh – as in dharma
n – as in nut

Semivowels
y – as in yes
r – as in run

l – as in light
v – as in vine
Aspirate
h – as in home

Sibilants
ś – as in ship, wish;
s – as in sun
Anusvara
ṅ – a resonant nasal sound as in numb
Visarga
ḥ – a final h-sound pronounced like aha
Special
ṛ – as in ridder